# 100
## YEARS OF
## MOTORSPORT

# 100
# YEARS OF
# MOTORSPORT

PA Photos

AMMONITE
**PRESS**

First published 2008 by

**AMMONITE PRESS**

an imprint of AE Publications Ltd.

166 High Street, Lewes, East Sussex BN7 1XU

ISBN 978-1-906672-03-4

British Cataloguing in Publication Data. A catalogue record of this book is available from the British Library.

Editor **NEIL DUNNICLIFFE**
Designer **JO PATTERSON**

Colour origination by GMC Reprographics
Printed and bound by Colorprint Offset in China

# Contents

# Chapter One

# PEOPLE

# THE GREAT AND GOOD

## Motorsport has always attracted strong characters, both on and off the track

The list of eminent motorsport personalities is both long and illustrious, and isn't confined to the track. Britain has produced some of the finest designers such as Adrian Newey and Patrick Head, innovators like Colin Chapman, world class team bosses like Ron Dennis, race doctors in the form of Syd Watkins, and commentators like Murray Walker.

That pedigree extends through the ranks, at all levels of British motorsport, right down to our volunteer marshals. Not all of these are represented on these pages but they should feel free to bathe in the reflected glory of those who are.

KAY PETRE (R) AND JOAN RICHMOND (L) GIVE A RILEY AN OVERHAUL. 15/06/1933

### EARLY DAYS

The early days of motorsport produced a special breed of driver with only one goal in mind: sheer speed. Their competitive instinct was directed more towards beating the stopwatch, rather than competitive racing. The drivers themselves also played a huge role in designing and modifying their own cars.

Brooklands was highly significant in the history of women in motorsport from the moment it opened, in June 1907, with a procession of cars headed by an Itala driven by Ethel Locke-King, wife of Brooklands founder Sir Hugh Fortescue Locke-King. Women drivers were already prominent: Dorothy Levitt had made a name for herself driving a Napier to win the Challenge Trophy at the 1905 Brighton speed trials.

In 1908 Brooklands permitted women to race, opening the door for the 1920s and 1930s heroines like the courageous Gwenda Hawkes who drove an ambulance on the Russian front in the Great War. Other favourites at Brooklands were Canadian Kay Petre in her pale blue Bugatti and matching overalls, 'Flying Fay' Taylour, and Mildred Bruce who had been the first woman ever to appear in court on a speeding charge, at Bow Street Magistrates Court in 1911, aged just 15.

Early male drivers repeatedly set new standards, in particular Selwyn Edge,

STIRLING MOSS. 01/03/1954

Kennelm Lee Guinness, Major Henry Segrave, Malcolm Campbell and Count Louis Zborowski. Born in Mayfair, as befitted his aristocratic bloodline, Zborowski typified the combined driver and automotive engineer. He built the 27 litre Higham Special, later known as 'Babs', which was used by J.G. Parry-Thomas in his fatal world land speed record attempt at Pendine Sands in 1927. Louis Zborowski himself died after his Mercedes hit a tree during the Italian Grand Prix.

## BETWEEN THE WARS

This period between the two World Wars saw competitive racing branch off from speed and endurance events and a different kind of driver gradually emerged, perhaps epitomised by the legendary Tazio Nuvolari. One of the British characters to emerge was Reg Parnell who started racing in 1935. His driving style would be described by some as totally committed, by others as wild.

## THE FIFTIES

Foremost in everyone's mind from the 1950s are some of the truly great names in world motorsport: Stirling Moss, Mike Hawthorn and John Surtees. Stirling Moss made his F1 debut in 1951 but didn't win a race until the 1955 British Grand Prix, finishing second in the title race that year to fellow Mercedes driver Juan Manuel Fangio. For the next two seasons Fangio pipped him to the post again for the title, as did Mike Hawthorn in 1958. In 1962 his competitive driving career was brought to a premature end with an horrific crash at Goodwood. Sir

NIGEL MANSELL. 06/10/1985

Stirling received his knighthood in 2000 in recognition of his past and continuing contributions to motorsport. Mike Hawthorn won the world title once, in 1958 for Ferrari. That title race went down to the wire with the last race in Morocco being the decider between Hawthorn and Moss.

## THE SIXTIES

In the 1960s Jim Clark, Graham Hill and John Surtees rose to prominence, with Jackie Stewart to follow at the end of the decade.

Jim Clark joined Lotus in 1960 and forged a phenomenal partnership with innovative team boss Colin Chapman, winning the British Grand Prix four years in succession and five times in total. He won the F1 world title in 1963 and again in 1965, also winning the British Touring Car Championship in the year between.

Graham Hill, father of Damon, succeeded in winning the F1 world title in 1962 and 1968 and remains the only driver to have completed the winning treble of F1 World Championship, Indy 500 and Le Mans.

The 1968 F1 season was also remarkable for something which was to change the face of racing forever: commercial sponsorship.

John Surtees won his first motorcycling world championship in 1956 and followed it with six more before signing for Colin Chapman at Lotus in 1960, going on to win the 1964 F1 drivers' championship. He will be remembered as the only person to win world championships on both two wheels and four.

By this time another Scot had risen in the ranks of the world's greatest drivers: Jackie Stewart. From an early age he displayed a natural talent and was quickly spotted by Ken Tyrrell who signed him to drive in Formula Three in 1964, but Formula One beckoned and Jackie Stewart was soon on his way to BRM. He rejoined the Tyrrell team in 1968 where he stayed until his retirement, having won three world titles with them in 1969, 1971 and 1973.

## THE SEVENTIES

The dashing figure of James Hunt made its way up through the ranks of Formula Ford, F3 and F2 to make his F1 debut in 1973. Hunt moved to McLaren for 1976 and spent the year battling with teammate Niki Lauda, eventually winning his only world title. James Hunt quit racing in 1979 and took up a new role as television commentator.

## EIGHTIES AND NINETIES

The 1980s were the years that gave Nigel Mansell the grounding necessary for his long-awaited F1 world championship title in 1992. Mansell had spent the first four years with Lotus after joining them in 1980, then moved to Williams – the team he is most associated with. His disintegrating front tyre in Australia, during the last race of the 1986 season, robbed him of the world championship and is an image many of us will never forget. But two years later he finished only two races all season and, frustrated, he moved to Ferrari

for two years. Fortunately for Williams, he returned to their camp and in 1992 they were rewarded with the constructors' championship while Mansell took the drivers' world title. He is one of a handful of people who have been awarded the BBC Sports Personality of the Year Award twice, in 1986 when he almost won the world championship and in 1992 when he finally succeeded.

With Nigel Mansell's retirement from F1, Graham Hill's son Damon stepped into the breach, hotly pursued by David Coulthard and then Jenson Button. Damon Hill won the world title in 1996 with Williams but left the team at the season's end.

## A NEW MILLENNIUM

Meanwhile, a young man from Doncaster was quietly chipping away at a different world championship. James Toseland first competed in the World Superbike Championship in 2001 and won it for the first time in 2004, repeating the title win in 2007. But the attention of the public was elsewhere. For the first time since

Damon Hill's 1996 title win, the 2007 F1 season witnessed a universally popular British driver come within a whisker of winning that same championship, and all in his rookie year. Lewis Hamilton fever had gripped the nation.

LEWIS HAMILTON. 15/01/2007

**OPPOSITE**

COUNT L. ZBOROWSKI IN HIS ASTON

MARTIN. 21/10/1921

A. DENLY, MOTORCYCLIST. 06/04/1925

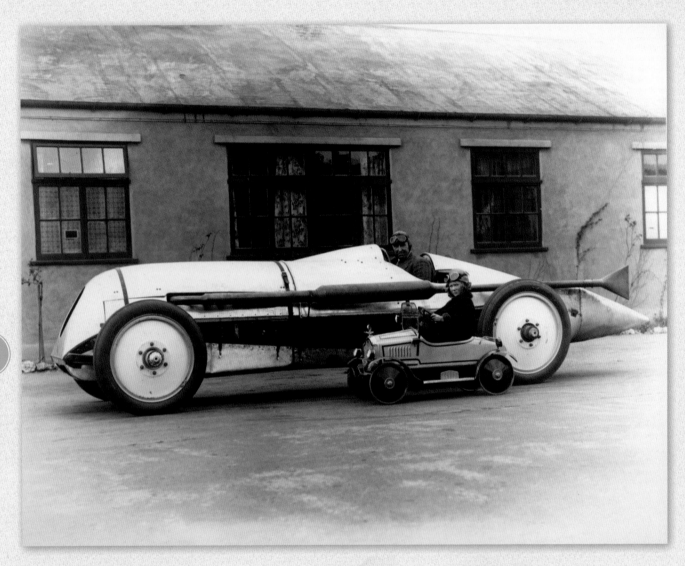

JOHN PARRY THOMAS AND MISS
ANNE DUKE WILLIAMS IN THEIR
RESPECTIVE VEHICLES. 18/04/1925

**OPPOSITE**

MISS IVY CUMMINS IN HER BUGATTI.
09/06/1925

**OPPOSITE**

MAJOR H.O.D. SEGRAVE (L), AFTER
WINNING THE 200 MILE RACE AT
BROOKLANDS. COUNT G. MASETTI,
WHO CAME SECOND, IS ON THE
RIGHT. 26/09/1925

LOUIS WAGNER, WINNER OF THE
FIRST BRITISH GRAND PRIX.
07/08/1926

KAY PETRE IN HER BUGATTI AT BROOKLANDS. 16/03/1930

J.S. WRIGHT WEARING AN AERODYNAMICALLY STYLED HELMET. 19/04/1931

GEORGE EYSTON ON THE TRACK AT MONTLHERY. 1932

**OPPOSITE**

TAZIO NUVOLARI IN A BUGATTI. 1932

CHAPTER ONE · PEOPLE

J.H. BERGER RELAXES AT THE WHEEL.
06/06/1932

**OPPOSITE**

SIR HENRY BIRKIN. 1932

**OPPOSITE**

THE TWO CAPTAINS, JACK PARKER,
ENGLAND (L) AND FRANK ARTHUR,
AUSTRALIA (R), PRIOR TO THE
ENGLAND AND AUSTRALIA SPEEDWAY
TEST MATCH AT CRYSTAL PALACE.
06/08/1932

GEORGE DULLER, THE FAMOUS
JOCKEY-AIRMAN-MOTORIST.
24/09/1932

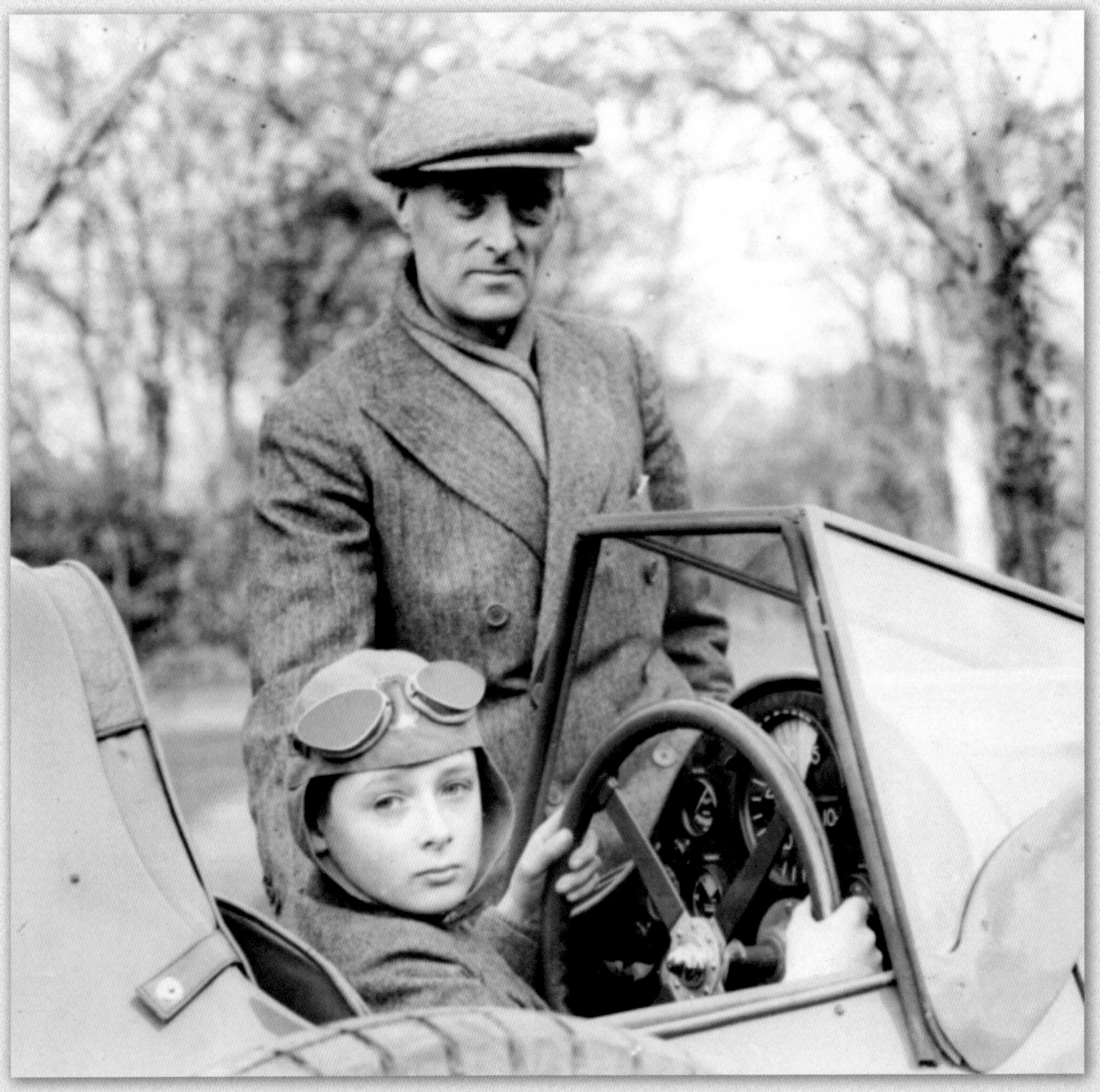

TIGER STEVENSON, WEST HAM.
09/05/1933

TAZIO NUVOLARI. 09/10/1933

ERIC FERNIHOUGH ON AN EXCELSIOR
J.A.P. 175 CC MOTORCYCLE, AT
BROOKLANDS. 31/10/1933

F.M. BARRADELL, DIRT TRACK RACER. 06/04/1934

**OPPOSITE**

KAYE DON SPLASHES THROUGH A
PUDDLE OF WATER IN HIS ALFA
ROMEO. 28/04/1934

HARRY ROSE PASSES BY THE
BROOKLANDS HANGER. 29/06/1935

**OPPOSITE**

DOREEN EVANS IN HER SINGLE
SEATER RACING MG. 18/04/1935

W.R. BAIRD. 21/09/1935

**OPPOSITE**

R.C. FLEMING LOOKS AROUND TO
MAKE SURE NO PHOTOGRAPHERS
ARE LURKING IN HIS BLIND SPOT
BEHIND HIS MG. 28/04/1936

LIONEL VAN PRAAG. 09/05/1936

**OPPOSITE**

DOREEN EVANS TAKING

REFRESHMENT. 28/05/1936

NEVILLE LLOYD PRACTISES AT BROOKLANDS IN HIS MG. 31/08/1936

**OPPOSITE**

HANS RUESCH (L) AND HIS
CO-DRIVER DICK SEAMAN (R)
CELEBRATE VICTORY WITH A GLASS
OF CHAMPAGNE. 30/10/1936

MORIAN HANSEN, HACKNEY WICK.
31/05/1937

**OPPOSITE**

GEORGE NEWTON, NEW CROSS.

22/05/1937

A BROOKLANDS MECHANIC FASTENS
THE BUCKLE ON MISS D. TURNER'S
HELMET. 10/07/1937

**OPPOSITE**

KAY PETRE SITS IN THE COCKPIT OF
HER CAR. 01/10/1937

BERT HADLEY PREPARES TO RELEASE THE HANDBRAKE ON HIS AUSTIN TO BEGIN
HIS ATTEMPT AT THE STANDING MILE RECORD AT BROOKLANDS. 12/10/1937

**OPPOSITE**

NOEL POPE JUMPS THE BANKING ON
HIS MOTORCYCLE. 08/05/1938

**OPPOSITE**

OLIVER BERTRAM SITS AT THE WHEEL
OF HIS BARNATO-HASSAN AS TWO
FRIENDS GIVE HIM A HELPFUL PUSH
AT BROOKLANDS. 20/05/1938

OLIVER BERTRAM RISES OFF THE
TRACK AT SPEED IN HIS BARNATO-
HASSAN. 20/05/1938

CORDY MILNE, BRISTOL. 23/07/1938

**OPPOSITE**

A.C. DOBSON TUNES UP HIS CAR'S
ENGINE, WITH HELP FROM HIS WIFE.
17/03/1939

MISS PATTEN (BARONESS DORNDORF) SITS ON THE DOOR OF HER PEUGEOT OUTSIDE TOM KNOWLES' GARAGE.
06/05/1939

A. BARON (BUGATTI) AND JACK BARLETT (ALFA ROMEO) RACE TOGETHER IN FRONT OF A SCRUBBED BROOKLANDS HANGER. 31/05/1939

(L-R) CUTH HARRISON (ERA B) LEADS
BOB GERARD (ERA B) AROUND A
BEND. 08/05/1947

**OPPOSITE**

SIR MALCOLM CAMPBELL SITTING IN
THE COCKPIT OF BLUEBIRD.
01/05/1947

STIRLING MOSS (L) IN HIS HWM
SHAKES HANDS WITH LOUIS ROSIER.
05/05/1951

**OPPOSITE**

WIMBLEDON'S RONNIE MOORE (L)
HAS A LAUGH WITH WEMBLEY'S
BRUCE ABERNETHY. 27/06/1951

JUAN MANUEL FANGIO (R) AND STIRLING MOSS (L) WISH EACH OTHER GOOD
LUCK BEFORE THEIR RACE. 14/04/1952

**OPPOSITE**

CHARLES COOPER (L) AND HIS SON
JOHN (R) WITH THEIR COOPER-
BRISTOL 2000CC RACING CAR.
16/04/1952

JUAN MANUEL FANGIO OF
ARGENTINA DRIVING A MASERATI
DURING PRACTICE AT AINTREE.
17/05/1953

**OPPOSITE**

REG BICKNELL AT HIGH SPEED IN HIS
ERSKINE STARIDE. 11/07/1953

STIRLING MOSS. 17/06/1954

JOHN SURTEES IN HIS FIRST YEAR WITH A FACTORY TEAM – NORTON. SURTEES WAS TO WIN SEVEN WORLD CHAMPIONSHIPS ON TWO WHEELS BEFORE SWITCHING TO FOUR, WITH LOTUS, AT THE END OF THE DECADE. 20/06/1955

STIRLING MOSS (R) WITH AMERICAN DRIVER PHIL HILL (L). 05/09/1957

BELLE VUE RIDER PETER CRAVEN.
16/09/1957

JOHN SURTEES RIDING AN MV AGUSTA 350CC. 31/07/1958

**OPPOSITE**

MARIA TERESA DE FILIPPIS IN HER

MASERATI AT SILVERSTONE.

02/05/1959

DONALD CAMPBELL SITS IN THE COCKPIT OF HIS NEW BLUEBIRD CN7/62, IN
WHICH HE WAS TO BREAK THE WORLD LAND SPEED RECORD IN 1964. 02/07/1960

**OPPOSITE**

STIRLING MOSS AT BRANDS HATCH.

*25/08/1960*

MIKE HAILWOOD. 29/04/1961

**OPPOSITE**

GRAHAM HILL IN RACING OVERALLS.

01/06/1963

**OPPOSITE**

LOTUS DRIVER JIM CLARK (L) SEEKS
ADVICE FROM MOTOR RACING
LEGEND STIRLING MOSS (R).
10/07/1964

JACKIE STEWART. 30/03/1965

**OPPOSITE**

JIM CLARK SITS IN HIS LOTUS 30

FORD. 28/08/1964

JIM CLARK SEATED IN HIS LOTUS AT
BRANDS HATCH. 01/04/1965

**OPPOSITE**

JOHN SURTEES SEATED IN HIS CAR AT BRANDS HATCH. 01/04/1965

JOHN SURTEES, SEATED IN A LOLA

BMW AT SILVERSTONE. *27/03/1967*

OPPOSITE

BRIAN WADE ON A GREEVES IN THE
INTERNATIONAL MOTO-CROSS
GRAND PRIX AT DODINGTON PARK,
GLOUCESTERSHIRE. 11/08/1968

JACKIE STEWART TRIES HIS HAND AT PLAYING THE TROMBONE WHILE SITTING
IN HIS MATRA FORD, WATCHED BY CHRIS BARBER (R) AND HIS JAZZ BAND.
14/03/1969

DEREK BELL. 18/07/1969

TYRRELL TEAM BOSS KEN TYRRELL (R)
WITH HIS STAR DRIVER JACKIE
STEWART (L) AND THE TYRRELL FORD.
01/03/1970

MIKE HAILWOOD. 01/10/1971

**OPPOSITE**

JACKIE STEWART. 04/04/1971

JACKIE STEWART ON HIS WAY TO VICTORY IN THE MONACO GRAND PRIX IN HIS
TYRRELL FORD.  03/06/1973

**OPPOSITE**

BARRY SHEENE. 05/08/1973

JAMES HUNT. 19/07/1974

JODY SCHECKTER AT THE BRITISH GRAND PRIX. 20/07/1974

DAVINA GALICA AT THE PRESS CONFERENCE WHERE SHE ANNOUNCED THAT SHE WOULD BE SWITCHING SPORTS, FROM SKIING TO MOTOR RACING. 13/02/1975

**OPPOSITE**

EVEL KNIEVEL ENTERTAINS THE CROWD AT WEMBLEY STADIUM BEFORE THE MAIN EVENT OF HIS PERFORMANCE, AN ATTEMPT TO JUMP OVER 13 DOUBLE DECKER BUSES ON HIS HARLEY DAVIDSON. 26/05/1975

NIKI LAUDA, FERRARI, AT PRACTICE
FOR THE BRITISH GRAND PRIX.
18/07/1975

PHIL READ ON A YAMAHA. 16/04/1976

JAMES HUNT IN HIS MARLBORO
MCLAREN M23. 18/07/1976

PHIL READ. 08/04/1977

BARRY SHEENE (L) AND PAT HENNEN
(R) LINE UP ON THE GRID AT BRANDS
HATCH. 24/03/1978

**OPPOSITE**

NIKI LAUDA, FERRARI, AT THE BRITISH
GRAND PRIX. 16/07/1977

MIKE HAILWOOD GIVES A THUMBS UP
AS HE POSES PRIOR TO HIS
COMPETITIVE MOTORCYCLING
COMEBACK. 04/05/1978

**OPPOSITE**

EDDIE KIDD POSING IN FRONT OF
THE 14 DOUBLE DECKER BUSES
WHICH HE ATTEMPTED TO JUMP TO
BREAK EVEL KNIEVEL'S WORLD
DISTANCE RECORD. 08/04/1978

FERRARI'S GILLES VILLENEUVE LEADS
FROM RENAULT'S JEAN-PIERRE
JABOUILLE IN THE BRITISH GRAND
PRIX. 16/07/1978

**OPPOSITE**

LOTUS BOSS COLIN CHAPMAN (L)
TALKS TO MARIO ANDRETTI (IN CAR)
PRIOR TO THE START OF THE BRITISH
GRAND PRIX. 16/07/1978

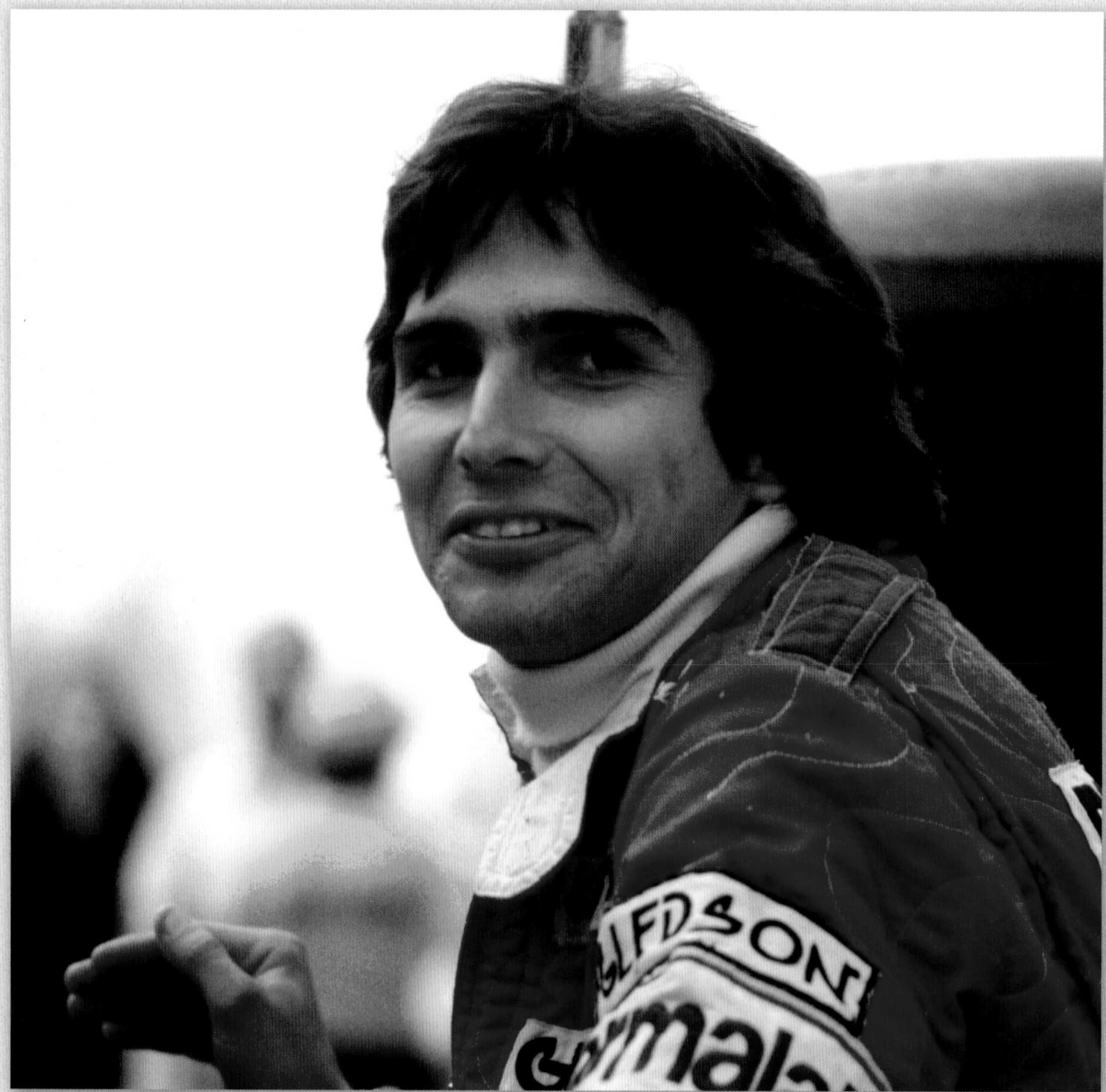

BARRY SHEENE. 10/03/1981

FREDDIE SPENCER IN ACTION. 31/07/1983

DAMON HILL AND HIS MOTHER,
BETTE, PERCH ON HIS CAR AFTER HE
SIGNED A CONTRACT TO DRIVE IN
THE FORMULA FORD CHAMPIONSHIP.
01/08/1984

WILLIAMS BOSS FRANK WILLIAMS (L) TALKS TO NIGEL MANSELL (R) BEFORE THE
START OF THE EUROPEAN GRAND PRIX AT BRANDS HATCH. 06/10/1985

**OPPOSITE**

ALAIN PROST CELEBRATES BECOMING
WORLD CHAMPION AT BRANDS
HATCH.  06/10/1985

JOEY DUNLOP, NORTHERN IRELAND'S WORLD MOTORCYCLE ROAD RACING CHAMPION, OUTSIDE BUCKINGHAM PALACE IN LONDON BEFORE HE RECEIVED AN MBE FROM THE PRINCE OF WALES. 07/03/1986

JACKIE STEWART (L) WITH MCLAREN DRIVER ALAIN PROST (R), WHO OVERTOOK THE
SCOT'S RECORD OF 27 GRANDS PRIX WINS LATER IN THE 1987 SEASON. 10/07/1987

EDDIE IRVINE AND EDDIE JORDAN.
27/06/1997

**OPPOSITE**

NIGEL MANSELL WINKS AT THE
CAMERA. 27/02/1992

CARL FOGARTY. 03/08/1997

**OPPOSITE**

JACQUES VILLENEUVE AT THE BRITISH
GRAND PRIX. 12/07/1997

THE MITSUBISHI DRIVEN BY RICHARD BURNS IN ACTION DURING THE SAFARI
RALLY IN NAIROBI. BURNS WON THE RALLY AND FINLAND'S JUHA KANKKUNEN,
IN A FORD ESCORT, WAS SECOND. 02/03/1998

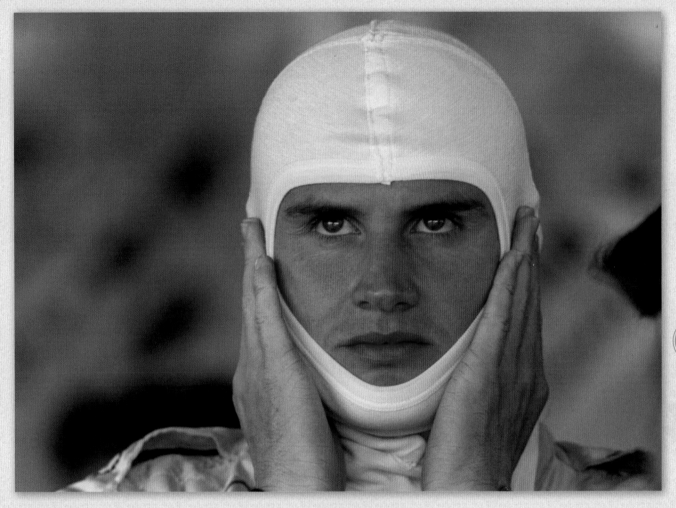

DAVID COULTHARD PREPARES FOR QUALIFYING AT THE 1998 AUSTRALIAN
GRAND PRIX. 06/03/1998

BERNIE ECCLESTONE (L) TALKS TO FERRARI TEAM BOSS JEAN TODT (R). 06/03/1998

WILLIAMS TEAM BOSS FRANK WILLIAMS. 25/09/1998

MCLAREN TECHNICAL DIRECTOR ADRIAN NEWEY CHATS TO TEAM BOSS RON DENNIS. 26/09/1998

CARL FOGARTY. 02/05/1999

MICHAEL SCHUMACHER WATCHES THE TIMES DURING PRACTICE AT THE BRITISH GRAND PRIX. 21/04/2000

FERRARI'S MICHAEL SCHUMACHER AT THE BRITISH GRAND PRIX. 23/04/2000

FRANK WILLIAMS, WITH THE
WILLIAMS TEAM GATHERED BEHIND
HIM. 15/06/2000

**OPPOSITE**

MURRAY WALKER – THE VOICE OF
FORMULA ONE – WHO RETIRED FROM
COMMENTATING AT THE END OF THE
2001 SEASON. 11/12/2000

RON DENNIS, MCLAREN TEAM BOSS. 16/03/2002

EDDIE JORDAN. 17/07/2002

PEOPLE

123

CHAPTER ONE

SIR JACKIE STEWART. 11/07/2004

LEWIS HAMILTON IN THE PITS DURING A PRACTICE SESSION AHEAD OF THE HUNGARIAN GRAND PRIX. 03/08/2007

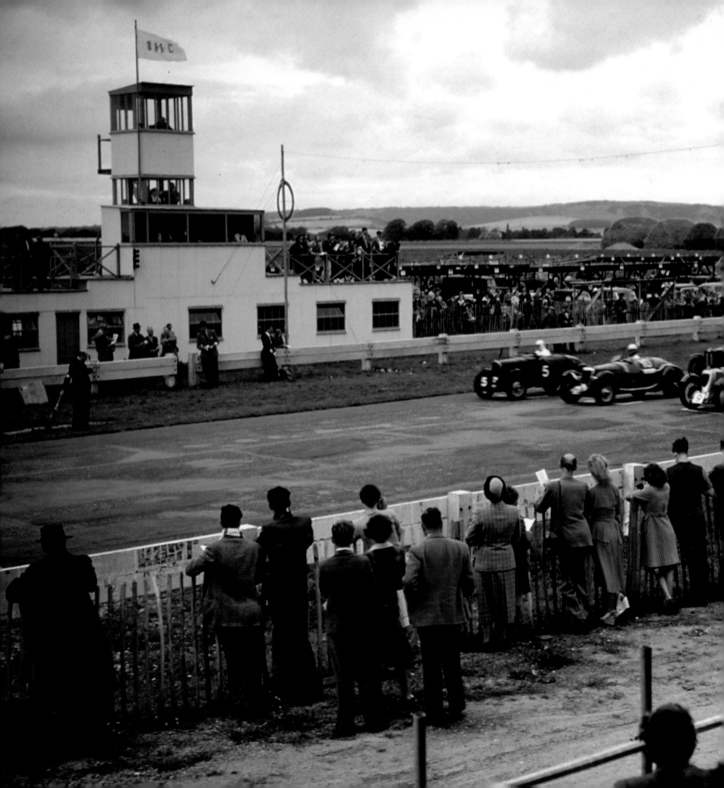

# Chapter Two
# PLACES

# TRACKS AND VENUES

## The best tracks combine history, atmosphere and style with raw noise and pure excitement

The history, development and pioneering spirit evident on these pages illustrates as solid a foundation for motorsport today as the brickyard at Indianapolis.

Brooklands stands out as being the best documented of our early motorsport venues but it isn't the oldest. Bexhill-on-Sea claims to be the birthplace of British motor racing with an inaugural straight-line race meeting in 1902. Ambitious plans were drawn up for the creation of a circuit there but they were never realised.

In 1905 Brighton's first stretch of tarmacadam road, now Madeira Drive, was created for the specific purpose of holding a series of motor races. A Napier, driven by Selwyn Edge, recorded a top speed in excess of 90mph and was a clear promise of excitement to come. Brooklands, which opened in 1907, was to be the setting for much of that excitement.

### BROOKLANDS

When Brooklands opened for business on its Weybridge Heath site it provided a range of possibilities: three different track permutations and several different finish lines. In fact, its original

CARS FILE INTO THE PADDOCK AT BROOKLANDS AFTER A RACE. 22/04/1935

purpose wasn't so much a racetrack as a test track. The main layout was the now famous oval with a special finishing straight and its infamous banking at each end, reaching a maximum of nearly 30ft in height.

To help establish Brooklands' reputation, shortly after its opening Selwyn Edge attempted a 24 hour endurance trial in his Napier, aiming for an average speed of 60mph. He succeeded, with an average of just below 66mph, driving 1581 miles in the process.

After the Great War, Brooklands re-opened in 1920 and by the end of the decade it had witnessed a number of momentous events including the 1926 and 1927 British Grands Prix. Race distances at the famous oval circuit were to climb from 200 miles in the 1920s to 500 and even 800 miles in length during the 1930s.

Motorcycle racing and record attempts were also features at Brooklands during this period, along with endurance events like the Double Twelve Race which was a 24 hour race split into two 12 hour daylight sessions. As early as 1921 Kennelm Lee Guinness had unofficially clocked 140mph at Brooklands and established a lap record in excess of 120mph, both of which he was to surpass, officially, the following season in his aero-engined V12 Sunbeam.

Other famous faces seen at Brooklands during this era were Major Henry Segrave and Count Louis Zborowski. Segrave won the Brooklands 200 Mile Race three times in 1921, 1925 and 1926 and was knighted after breaking Campbell's land speed record for the first time in 1927. Meanwhile, Count Zborowski built a reputation at Brooklands for driving aero-engined cars with immense power.

## CRYSTAL PALACE

In 1927 a circuit was established at Crystal Palace. The first race, for motorcycles, used a one-mile course on existing footpaths in the park; subsequently a speedway track was built and used between 1928 and 1934. Speedway was proving immensely popular with Londoners, a natural progression from early motorcycle races on grass and gravel. Plans were drawn up for a two-mile Grand Prix circuit at Crystal Palace in 1935 but the following year it was destroyed by fire. Undeterred, work began on the track just days after the catastrophe, using a revolutionary non-skid surface.

In July 1937 Crystal Palace hosted the London Grand Prix, which was won in an ERA by Prince Birabongse from Bangkok, who had come to the UK to attend Eton and Cambridge. Racing continued at Crystal Palace until the outbreak of war, not too resume until 1953. Its last international meeting took place in May 1972, with Mike Hailwood setting a lap record of over 103mph, and in 1974 the circuit finally closed for good.

Perhaps the most significant event in Crystal Palace's history, given what was to become the norm decades later, took place on 9 October 1937. This was the first live broadcast of a motorsport event by the BBC, which covered the International Imperial Trophy Race.

### DONINGTON PARK

By this time a permanent track had been constructed at Donington Park, opening in 1933. The initial 2.18 mile track was extended in its second year by 600 yards and racing cars were added to the programme. The first Donington Grand Prix was held in 1935 (permission to call it the British Grand Prix was denied) but the British Grand Prix did take place there in 1937 and 1938, the latter being won by the legendary Tazio Nuvolari.

The circuit was shortly to become a wartime military vehicle depot.

However, it was purchased and rebuilt in the 1970s and has since established itself as a popular venue for the British Touring Car Championship, British Superbikes and MotoGP. It was also the setting for one of the late Ayrton Senna's greatest F1 performances during the European Grand Prix on Easter Sunday of 1993, the first GP at Donington since Nuvolari won in 1938.

### AINTREE

In the same year that Crystal Palace resumed racing, 1953, another venue was about to rise to prominence:

Aintree, home of the Grand National. Just like Crystal Palace, it already had a high public profile and, with existing grandstands and other infrastructure in place, it was able to rise in prominence and popularity very quickly. In 1954 it hosted the Daily Telegraph Aintree 200 which was won by Stirling Moss as a precursor to winning the British Grand Prix at Aintree in 1955 in his Mercedes W196, beating Juan Manuel Fangio in another Mercedes.

The circuit also hosted the 1957 British Grand Prix again won by Moss, now driving for Vanwall, who shared the car with Tony Brooks. Aintree also held the 1959, 1961 and 1962 British Grands Prix.

### SILVERSTONE

The RAC, several years earlier, had

SHANE BYRNE AT THE BRITISH SUPERBIKES RACE AT SILVERSTONE. 30/03/2003

negotiated a lease on an old bomber base in Northamptonshire: Silverstone. This was the venue for the very first Formula 1 World Championship race in 1950, attended by King George VI.

The following year the RAC transferred the lease to the British Racing Drivers' Club and Silverstone continued to be the sole home of the British Grand Prix until the Aintree race in 1955, after which the two circuits shared the event until Brands Hatch became a contender. Silverstone witnessed the first 160mph lap in a Grand Prix, by Keke Rosberg during the 1985 British GP. Silverstone has been the sole venue for the British Grand Prix since 1987.

## BRANDS HATCH

Brands Hatch was constructed in a natural amphitheatre, which added interest for both drivers and spectators. The location already had a long history, having been used for motorcycle racing on a three-quarter mile dirt track since the 1930s, but it was not until 1947 that any real attempt was made to create a proper circuit.

In the 1950s the track was given a new tarmac surface and extended twice, the world famous Druids Bend was added, and racing changed to a clockwise direction in front of a newly acquired grandstand.

STIRLING MOSS IN ACTION AT BRANDS HATCH. 25/08/1960

Finally, in 1960 it was ready to host a Formula One event, albeit a non-championship race, before being sold. Its new owners quickly brought the circuit up to Grand Prix standard, Aintree was dropped from the calendar, and from 1963 the British Grand Prix was to be shared by Silverstone and Brands for the next 23 years. Brands Hatch played host to two European Grands Prix, in 1983 and 1985 when Nigel Mansell recorded his first Grand Prix victory, one that he was to repeat the following year in the last ever British Grand Prix to be held at the circuit.

Celebrating the achievements of our top performers at the best tracks is right and proper. But we must also remember the less glamorous circuits which provide the up and coming stars of the future with opportunities to hone their skills.

**OPPOSITE**

THE COMPETITORS IN THE FIRST
SOUTH COAST MOTOR RALLY
CHAMPIONSHIP OUTSIDE WARNE'S
HOTEL IN WORTHING. 01/06/1905

THE HUGE ENGINE OF 600 HP WHICH
DROVE THE GIANT RACING CAR
WHICH COUNT ZBOROWSKI ENTERED
FOR EASTER MONDAY RACING AT
BROOKLANDS. 14/08/1920

RACING AT BROOKLANDS. 02/05/1925

**OPPOSITE**

THE START OF THE 200 MILE RACE AT

BROOKLANDS. 26/09/1925

CARS PARKED ON THE BANKING AT
BROOKLANDS. 04/06/1930

**OPPOSITE**

JACK DUNFEE FILLS UP AT THE
BROOKLANDS PETROL STATION.
29/07/1929

KAYE DON ATTEMPTS TO BREAK THE
THREE HOUR/500KM RECORD IN 'THE
CUB', ONE OF HIS THREE WORKS
SUNBEAMS, AT BROOKLANDS.
25/06/1930

SPECTATORS WATCH THE CARS
RACING AT BROOKLANDS. 16/10/1930

MALCOLM CAMPBELL, SEATED IN HIS
7.5HP AUSTIN ON DAYTONA BEACH,
JUST PRIOR TO BREAKING THE WORLD
SPEED RECORD FOR 'BABY' CARS.
10/02/1931

**OPPOSITE**

A PHOTOGRAPHER SNAPS A PICTURE
OF GEORGE EYSTON AS HE FLIES
PAST IN HIS MG DURING A SPEED
RECORD ATTEMPT AT BROOKLANDS.
13/03/1931

SIR HENRY BIRKIN AT BROOKLANDS.
01/05/1932

**OPPOSITE**

BRITISH RACING DRIVER GEORGE
EYSTON, ON THE TRACK AT
MONTLHERY, FRANCE. 1932

THE ENGLAND TEAM, SPEEDWAY
FIRST TEST MATCH, ENGLAND V
AUSTRALIA AT WEMBLEY STADIUM.
26/06/1933

**OPPOSITE**

(L-R) BRIAN LEWIS, JOHN COBB, TIM
ROSE-RICHARDS AND A.O. SAUNDER
DAVIS AT BROOKLANDS. 20/06/1932

C.H. WOOD CLIMBS THE COL DU
GALIBIER IN HIS ASTON MARTIN.
03/08/1933

**OPPOSITE**

J.C. ELIVES AND S.B. HAILWOOD IN
THEIR MGS ON BROOKLANDS'
BANKED CIRCUIT. 16/09/1933

SPEEDWAY RIDERS AT THEIR SECOND
JOB – STAGE TURNS IN THE CIRCUS.
16/10/1934

**OPPOSITE**

WAL PHILLIPS (L) AND GUS KUHN (R)
AT THE ALEXANDRA PALACE RINK.
19/02/1934

THE LADIES' LE MANS TEAM
PRACTISING FOR THE FAMOUS 24
HOUR RACE AT BROOKLANDS IN
THEIR MGS. 12/04/1935

**OPPOSITE**

THE CROWD AT BROOKLANDS, WITH SOME SPECTATORS STANDING ON THE
BONNETS OF THEIR CARS TO OBTAIN A BETTER VIEW OF THE TRACK. 22/04/1935

BOOKMAKERS TAKING BETS OFF THE CROWD AT BROOKLANDS. 22/04/1935

A LARGE CROWD WATCHES FROM THE SCAFFOLDING AND ROOF-BEAMS OF AN
UNFINISHED HOUSE AS R.R.K. MARKER DRIVES PAST IN HIS RAILTON DURING
THE BUGATTI CLUB HILL CLIMB AT NORTHWOOD HILLS. 25/07/1935

TIMEKEEPER A.V. EBBLEWHITE
INSPECTS THE CARS BEFORE THE RACE
BEGINS AT BROOKLANDS. 16/08/1936

**OPPOSITE**

COMPETITORS HIT THE BRAKES AS
THEY TURN INTO STADIUM DIP BEND
AT THE CRYSTAL PALACE ROAD
RACING CIRCUIT. 15/05/1937

MANFRED VON BRAUCHITSCH TAKES
OFF AS HE CRESTS A SLIGHT HILL AT
DONINGTON PARK. 10/10/1937

**OPPOSITE**

ENTHUSIASTS WATCHING THE RACE FROM THE EDGE OF THE BANKING AT
BROOKLANDS AS JOHN COBB HURTLES TOWARDS THEM IN HIS NAPIER
RAILTON. 18/09/1937

ERIC FERNIHOUGH ON HIS SUPERCHARGED STREAMLINED BROUGH SUPERIOR
MACHINE AT BROOKLANDS. 11/03/1938

**OPPOSITE**

THE STARTER WAVES HIS FLAG AS THE
RACE COMMENCES WITH A ROLLING
START AT BROOKLANDS. 07/05/1938

MOTORCYCLISTS RACING ON THE
CAMPBELL CIRCUIT AT BROOKLANDS.
08/05/1938

**OPPOSITE**

MRS A.C. LACE SIGNALS IN THE PITS
AT BROOKLANDS. 29/08/1938

**OPPOSITE**

BOB ANSELL PLOUGHS THROUGH
THE WATER ON THE BROOKLANDS
TRACK IN HIS ERA. 06/05/1939

THE START OF THE SOAP-BOX DERBY
AT BROOKLANDS. 16/07/1939

(L-R) LESLIE BROOKE (ERA B) LEADS
RAYMOND MAYS (ERA D-TYPE R4D)
THROUGH THE STREETS OF ST
HELIER. 08/05/1947

**OPPOSITE**

RON JOHNSON, CAPTAIN OF THE NEW CROSS TEAM, WARMING UP BEFORE
THE START OF ONE OF HIS RACES AT THE NEW CROSS SPEEDWAY STADIUM IN
LONDON. 18/04/1946

THE CARS LINE UP AT THE START OF
THE JCC INTERNATIONAL TROPHY,
JERSEY. 08/05/1947

**OPPOSITE**

THE START OF A FIVE LAP SCRATCH
RACE UP TO 1100CC AT GOODWOOD.
12/08/1950

ALBERTO ASCARI, IN HIS FERRARI AT SILVERSTONE. 26/08/1950

MOTOR RACING AT CRYSTAL PALACE. 11/07/1953

PETER COLLINS, DRIVING HIS FERRARI, ZIPS THROUGH COPSE CORNER, ON HIS
WAY TO WINNING THE BRITISH GRAND PRIX AT SILVERSTONE. 20/07/1958

**OPPOSITE**

JOHN SURTEES AT THE WHEEL OF A
FERRARI, PRACTISING ON THE
BRANDS HATCH CIRCUIT FOR THE
BRITISH GRAND PRIX. 09/07/1964

JIM CLARK (5), DAN GURNEY (7) AND
MIKE SPENCE (6) MOVE OFF FROM
THE START AT BRANDS HATCH.
13/03/1965

JOHN PATTERSON, IN A BRABHAM BT
10, TALKS OVER A PRACTICE RUN WITH
A TIMEKEEPER AT BRANDS HATCH,
PRIOR TO THE LMC RADIO LONDON
CAR MEETING. 18/06/1967

THE CRYSTAL PALACE CIRCUIT
DURING A CAR RACE, WITH THE
GRANDSTAND AND TIMEKEEPER'S
BOX. 09/09/1967

**OPPOSITE**

A LOTUS FORD, WITH AEROFOILS
FITTED, IN ACTION AT BRANDS
HATCH. 14/03/1969

BRITAIN'S JAMES HUNT DRIVING A MCLAREN (11) AND MARIO ANDRETTI IN A LOTUS (5) LEAD THE WAY DURING THE JAPANESE GRAND PRIX AT FUJI. 28/10/1976

(R-L) PAT HENNEN LEADS KENNY ROBERTS AND A SMALL GROUP OF RIDERS AROUND GRAHAM HILL BEND AT BRANDS HATCH. 24/03/1978

DAMON HILL REFLECTED IN THE
WINDOWS ABOVE THE PIT LANE AT
QUALIFYING FOR THE SPANISH
GRAND PRIX. 31/05/1996

**OPPOSITE**

DAMON HILL DRIVING ROUND
LOEWS CORNER DURING QUALIFYING
FOR THE MONACO GRAND PRIX.
18/05/1996

TROPHY ROOM, MCLAREN INTERNATIONAL FACTORY. 12/12/1996

**OPPOSITE**

COLIN MCRAE, SUBARU, DURING THE
SWEDISH RALLY. 10/02/1997

DAVID COULTHARD ON A LAP
AROUND THE MONTREAL CIRCUIT.
06/06/1998

MECHANICS AWAIT DAMON HILL'S PIT STOP AT THE ITALIAN GRAND PRIX.
13/09/1998

**OPPOSITE**

A SMALL CROWD WATCHES THE
TOURING CARS AT DONINGTON
PARK. 20/06/1999

RICHARD BURNS DURING TESTING IN THE FOREST OF DEAN AHEAD OF THE
NETWORK Q RALLY. 19/11/1999

**OPPOSITE**

MARK HIGGINS IN HIS VOLKSWAGEN
GOLF GTI AT SWEET LAMB. 22/11/1999

UMBRELLAS ARE UP IN THE WELSH MOUNTAINS AS JARMO KYTOLEHTO IN HIS
VAUXHALL MAKES HIS WAY THROUGH THE FOREST. 23/11/1999

**OPPOSITE**

MCLAREN'S DAVID COULTHARD IN
ACTION AT SUZUKA AS THE BIG
WHEEL LOOMS IN THE BACKGROUND.
12/10/2001

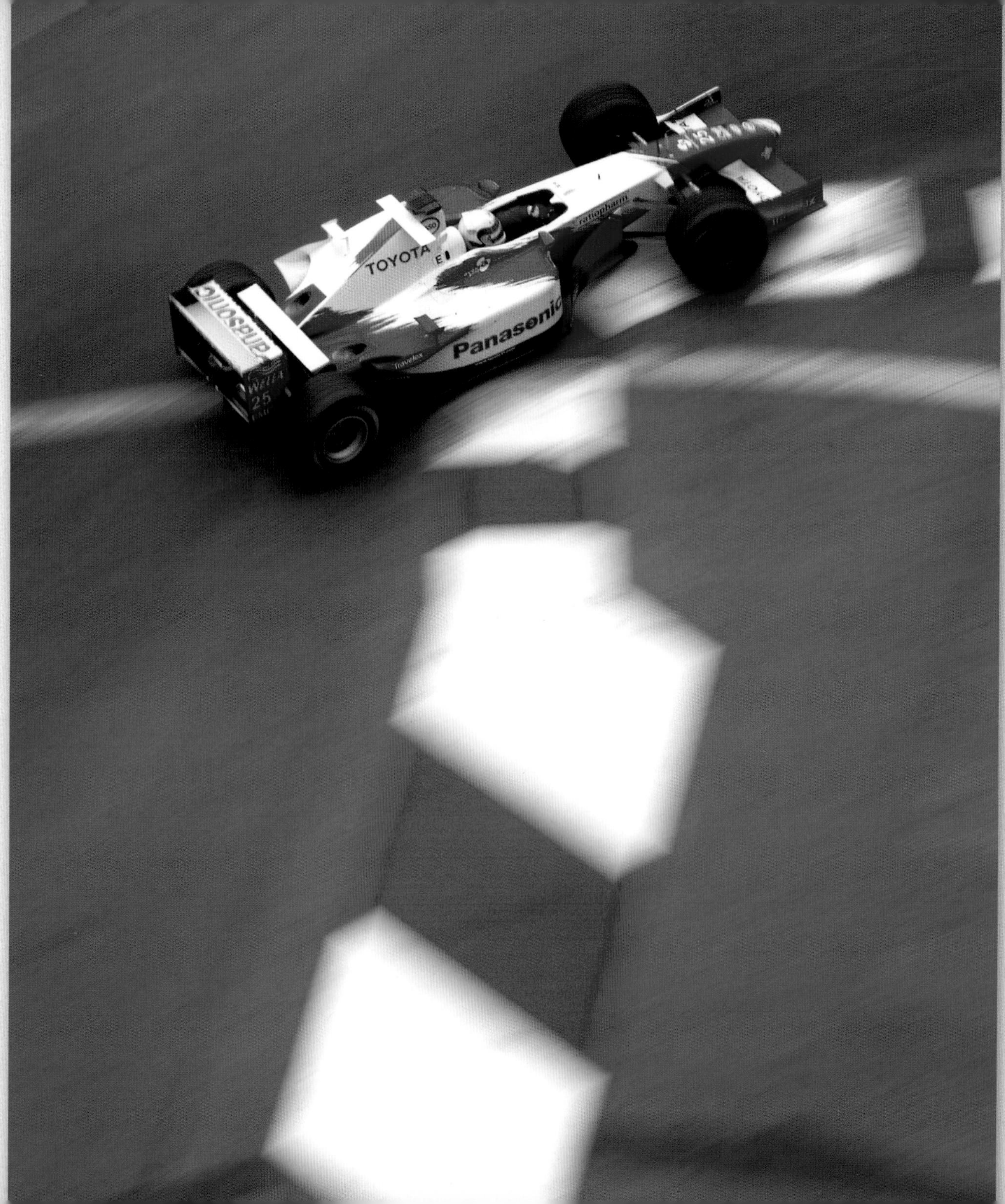
TOYOTA
Panasonic
ratiopharm
Travelex
WELLA
25

MCLAREN'S DAVID COULTHARD IN ACTION DURING QUALIFYING AT THE
MONACO GRAND PRIX. 25/05/2002

**OPPOSITE**

TOYOTA'S ALLAN MCNISH IN THE

PRACTICE SESSION IN MONTE CARLO.

23/05/2002

DAVID COULTHARD BLASTS DOWN THE START/FINISH STRAIGHT DURING
PRACTICE AT THE BRITISH GRAND PRIX. 05/07/2002

**OPPOSITE**

GIANCARLO FISICHELLA IN HIS
JORDAN AT SILVERSTONE.   26/02/2003

DAVID COULTHARD, DRIVING A MCLAREN MERCEDES, TAKES THE TURN ALONG REGENT STREET, LONDON, AS FORMULA ONE COMES TO THE CAPITAL DURING AN UNPRECEDENTED STREET MOTOR RACING EVENT. 06/07/2004

DAVID NORRIS OF GREAT BRITAIN AT THE MILLENNIUM STADIUM. 11/06/2005

NORWAY'S PETTER SOLBERG IN HIS SUBARU IMPREZA ON THE EPYNT SPECIAL
STAGE DURING THE WALES RALLY GREAT BRITAIN IN POWYS. 02/12/2006

**OPPOSITE**

MARCUS GRONHOLM IN A FORD
FOCUS WRC 06 DURING THE
TRAWSCOED STAGE OF THE WALES
RALLY GREAT BRITAIN IN
CARMARTHENSHIRE. 03/12/2006

LEWIS HAMILTON DURING A PRACTICE SESSION FOR THE BELGIAN GRAND PRIX
AT SPA-FRANCORCHAMPS. 15/09/2007

**OPPOSITE**

SWEDEN'S ANTONIO LINDBACK IN

ACTION AT THE MILLENNIUM

STADIUM. 30/06/2007

## Chapter Three
## MOMENTS

# TRAGEDIES AND TRIUMPHS

## Motorsport has had its share of successes and failures

FORMER WORLD RALLY CHAMPION, THE LATE COLIN MCRAE. 18/05/2006

**B**ritish motorsport has an enviable record when it comes to safety. While we must mourn the untimely passing of some of our greatest legends, it is a fact that most have passed away in accidents abroad or through circumstances other than racing incidents. The most recent tragedy of this nature is undoubtedly the helicopter crash which killed former world rally champion Colin McRae and his five-year old son. It also provided an eerie echo of the plane crash which killed Graham Hill and five of his team in 1975 in fog near Elstree.

The son of Jimmy McRae, five times British rally champion, Colin was the

first Briton to win this world championship in 1995 and was awarded the MBE the following year in recognition of his achievement. More recently, the Scot often did battle with Richard Burns, perhaps England's greatest rally driver. Burns was to become FIA World Rally Champion in 2001 but ceased racing two years later due to a brain tumour and passed away, to the exact day, on the fourth anniversary of winning his world title.

World 500cc Motorcycle Champion Barry Sheene died of throat and stomach cancer in Australia in 2003. He had moved there in the 1990s for a warmer climate due to the discomfort resulting from numerous broken bones from his racing accidents.

There have also been occasions when injuries sustained during a race have had fatal consequences after the event. The strangest of these involved Sir Henry "Tim" Birkin, famous for pioneering the "Blower Bentley" and for always wearing a blue and white spotted silk scarf when competing. Although racing a number of times in

the early 1920s, he began racing in earnest in 1927 in a 3 litre Bentley, then swapping to the 130 bhp 4.5 litre version. He supercharged this, increasing the power output to 242bhp, and later raised the Brooklands lap record to 133.88mph.

Several years after this, in May 1933 he competed in the Tripoli GP and made a pit stop while just 10 seconds behind Nuvolari. Wearing a short-sleeve shirt, he burned his bare forearm on a hot exhaust but made little of the incident, both at the time and afterwards. Sadly the burn turned septic and, lacking proper treatment, Birkin died of blood poisoning,

DAMON HILL ADJUSTS HIS BALACLAVA BEFORE PRACTICE AT THE BRITISH GRAND PRIX. 10/07/1998

although some reports have suggested it was really malaria.

**SAFETY**

Today's drivers are far better protected than in those days. One of the unsung heroes of the push to protect drivers from the consequences of accidents was Louis Stanley who created the Grand Prix medical service in 1967. He also helped to perfect the fireproof suits that all drivers must now wear.

The blackest year in British motor-sport was perhaps 1958, which saw the deaths of Luigi Musso and two British drivers: Peter Collins and Stuart Lewis-Evans.

Fatally, the Ferrari of Peter Collins left the Nurburgring track at 100mph. Team mate Hawthorn retired from the race immediately, and from racing completely at the end of the season.

That year also saw the death of Musso at the French GP, and of Stuart Lewis-Evans who crashed in Morocco in the final race of the season. Ironically, 29 year old Hawthorn was to lose his life in 1959 in a road accident on the Guildford by-pass, still not fully explained, after the season had ended.

## GREAT WINNERS

The 1957 British Grand Prix at Aintree, also classified as that season's Grand Prix de Europe, saw Stirling Moss win – unusually sharing his Vanwall with Tony Brooks – to achieve the first ever all-British car and driver combination to win a Formula 1 Grand Prix.

JIM CLARK IN ACTION IN HIS LOTUS CLIMAX AT THE BRITISH GRAND PRIX. 20/07/63

Sometimes greatness cannot be measured by statistics. Jim Clark established worldwide respect in only 72 Grand Prix starts. There are more GPs in the calendar now, drivers rarely participate in other formulae, and

than a third of the Grands Prix he started, beating Fangio in the number of races won, and was twice crowned World Champion, in 1963 and 1965. When he crashed into a tree at Hockenheim in a Formula 2 race in April 1968, he died instantly, cutting short a career which had brought joy and excitement to a generation of British motorsport enthusiasts.

## DISASTERS

Clark wasn't the only British driver to experience fatal consequences from crashing off the track. During the Italian Grand Prix of 1924 at Monza, the renowned British aristocrat Count Louis Zborowski suffered a similar fate when his 2 litre works Mercedes crashed into a tree at high speed.

Also Brooklands legends, Clive Dunfee and his younger brother Jack were racing an eight-litre Bentley in the Brooklands 500 Mile Race in 1932 when it rode too high on the banking and cart-wheeled off the circuit. Clive Dunfee, who had just taken over from Jack in a pit stop, was thrown clear but died instantly.

driver safety along with chassis integrity in crash situations are massively improved. Comparisons become rather meaningless, so Jim Clark is properly revered despite his relatively few races. He went on to win more

## ADVERSITY INTO TRIUMPH

There will always be people who turn adversity into triumph and team boss Frank Williams is a great example.

Driving home from the Paul Ricard circuit in France in 1986, he lost control of his car and suffered a broken neck in the ensuing crash. His life was in the balance for a while but he survived, paralysed from the chest down.

The Williams team still won the constructors' championship that year. A more realistic test of the team's character in the first full season since the team principal's accident, Williams went on to win the 1987 constructors' title almost doubling McLaren's points total in second place. They also took both first and second places in the drivers' championship that year, with Piquet and Mansell respectively.

Sir Frank Williams was awarded the CBE in 1987 and knighted in 1999. He is also one of few non-Frenchmen to be awarded the Légion d'honneur for his contribution to Renault.

MAJOR HENRY SEGRAVE IN
'SUNBEAM', THE CAR IN WHICH HE
WOULD GO ON TO BREAK THE
WORLD LAND SPEED RECORD IN
MARCH 1927 WITH AN AVERAGE
SPEED OF OVER 200MPH. 24/01/1927

L.J. ARCHER (L) LEADS FROM C.B. BICKELL (R) IN THE CHAMPION SCRATCH RACE CLASS B/S IN THE BRITISH MOTORCYCLE RACING CLUB MEET AT BROOKLANDS. 05/10/1929

KAYE DON'S SUNBEAM 'SILVER BULLET' AT SPEED DURING AN ATTEMPT ON THE WORLD LAND SPEED RECORD. 12/06/1930

THE 500 MILE RACE AT BROOKLANDS, WON BY S.C. DAVIS AND THE EARL OF MARCH IN AN AUSTIN CAR. THEY WON BY 10 MILES AT AN AVERAGE SPEED OF 83 MPH. HERE THE WINNING CAR PASSES THE POST. 05/10/1930

**OPPOSITE**

THE EARL OF MARCH AND C. S. STANILAND IN THEIR MG ON THE WAY TO VICTORY IN THE DOUBLE TWELVE RACE AT BROOKLANDS. THE EVENT WAS DIVIDED INTO TWO DAYLIGHT SESSIONS BECAUSE OF NOISE RESTRICTIONS AT NIGHT. THE WINNERS COVERED 601 LAPS AT AN AVERAGE SPEED OF 65.62 MPH. 09/05/1931

**OPPOSITE**

VAN DE BECKE TESTS THE £100
MORRIS MINOR, WHICH TRAVELS AT A
MAXIMUM SPEED OF 100MPH.
17/06/1931

SIR MALCOLM CAMPBELL'S BLUEBIRD
CAR, THE HOLDER OF THE WORLD
LAND SPEED RECORD, AT
BROOKLANDS. 20/04/1932

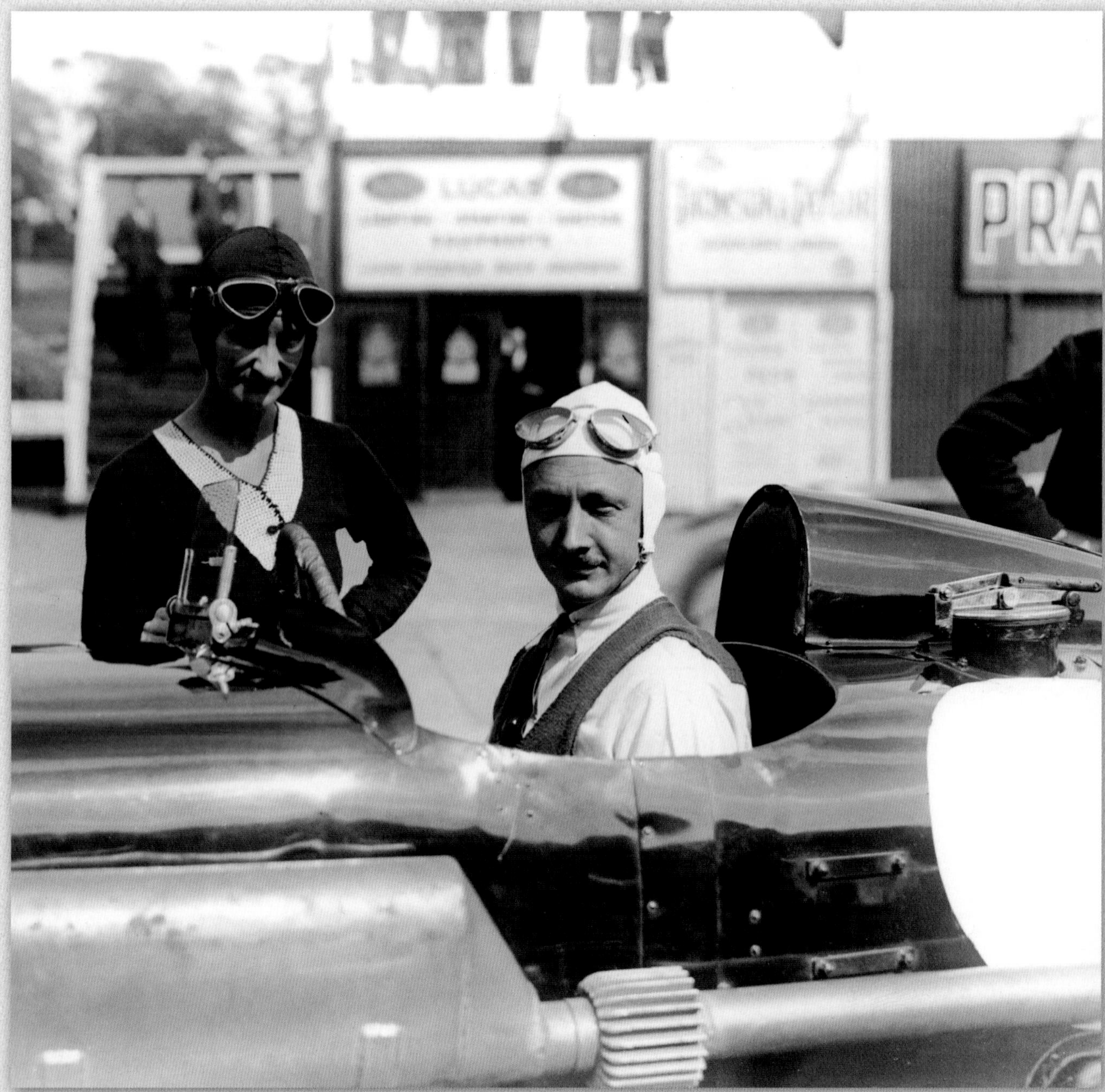
PRA

**OPPOSITE**

BROOKLANDS LAP RECORD HOLDER
SIR HENRY BIRKIN SITS IN HIS
BLOWER BENTLEY AND TALKS SHOP
WITH MRS ELSIE WISDOM.
01/06/1932

THE WORLD'S FASTEST LONG DISTANCE RACE – THE BRITISH RACING DRIVERS'
CLUB 500 MILES EVENT – TOOK PLACE AT BROOKLANDS. EVERY CAR ENTERED
HAD TO BE CAPABLE OF LAPPING THE TRACK AT 80MPH. 24/09/1932

THE TWO CAPTAINS, AUSTRALIA'S VIC
HUXLEY (L) AND ENGLAND'S HAROLD
'TIGER' STEVENSON (R), SHAKE
HANDS BEFORE THE SPEEDWAY FIRST
TEST MATCH BETWEEN ENGLAND
AND AUSTRALIA AT WEMBLEY
STADIUM. 26/06/1933

**OPPOSITE**

MALCOLM CAMPBELL'S RECORD
BREAKING BLUEBIRD, MINUS THE
BODYWORK, IS ROLLED INTO
OLYMPIA FOR THE FIRST DAY OF THE
MOTOR SHOW. 11/10/1933

JOHN COBB LEANS ON HIS CAR AFTER
BREAKING THE LAP RECORD AT
BROOKLANDS. 08/04/1934

**OPPOSITE**

JCC INTERNATIONAL TROPHY RACE WINNER WHITNEY STRAIGHT (C) SHAKES
HANDS WITH RUNNER UP BRIAN LEWIS (L) WHILE STRAIGHT'S MECHANIC
GUILIO RAMPONI LOOKS ON (R). 28/04/1934

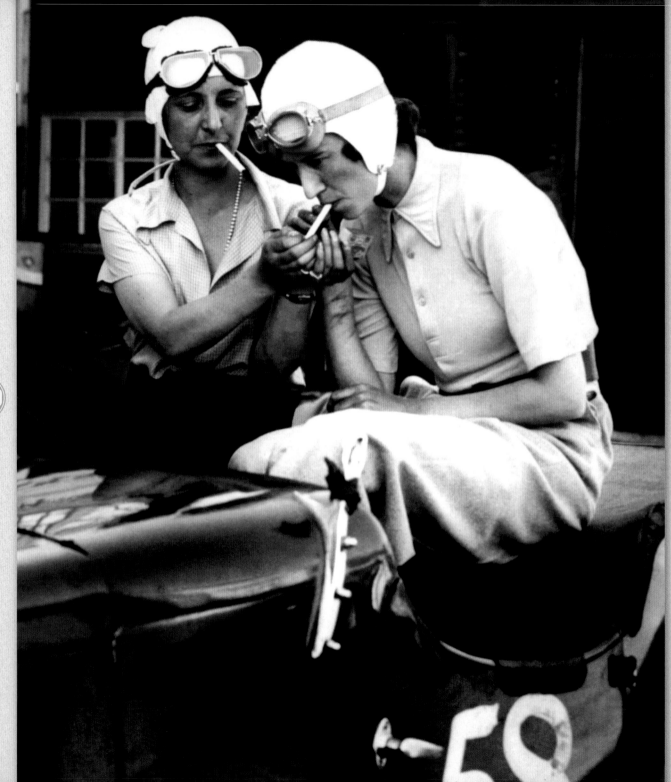

TIMEKEEPER A.V. EBBLEWHITE
INSPECTS THE BIKES BEFORE THE
RACE BEGINS AT BROOKLANDS.
05/08/1934

**OPPOSITE**

E. GORDON-SIMPSON (L) AND JOAN RICHMOND (R) BEFORE THE START OF THE
RACING AT BROOKLANDS. 07/07/1934

CARS LINE UP FOR THE START OF THE MOUNTAIN RACE AT BROOKLANDS. 21/09/1934

VICTOR STAFFORD'S STREAMLINED
CAR. 10/04/1935

THE WINNER OF THE BRITISH EMPIRE TROPHY RACE, DICK SEAMAN (C), STANDS ALONGSIDE THE RUNNER UP, PAT FAIRFIELD (L), AND THE THIRD PLACED DRIVER, BILL EVERITT (R). 04/04/1936

BRIAN DUCKER AND HIS PASSENGER NAVIGATE THE CORNER IN SPECTACULAR STYLE TO WIN THE SIDECAR SCRATCH RACE AT A GRASS TRACK MEETING AT BRANDS HATCH. 22/06/1936

WINNER OF THE 500 MILE RACE AT
BROOKLANDS, FREDERICK DIXON.
19/09/1936

**OPPOSITE**

THE RACE WINNER, RAYMOND MAYS
IN AN ERA, TAKES THE CHEQUERED
FLAG AT THE BRITISH EMPIRE TROPHY
RACE, DONINGTON PARK. 01/04/1937

**OPPOSITE**

H.L. BROOKE ATTENDS TO THE
ENGINE OF HIS MG RILEY AFTER
PLOUGHING INTO A FIELD AT
STARKEY'S CORNER DURING THE
NUFFIELD TROPHY AT DONINGTON
PARK. 12/06/1937

SMOKE BILLOWS FROM JOSEPH PAUL'S DELAGE AS BROOKLANDS OFFICIALS
FLOOD THE CAR WITH FIRE EXTINGUISHERS FOLLOWING ITS EXIT FROM THE
TRACK INTO THE CROWD DURING THE JCC INTERNATIONAL TROPHY AT
BROOKLANDS. 07/05/1938

JOSEPH PAUL IS CARRIED INTO AN AMBULANCE AFTER HIS HUGE CRASH
DURING THE JCC INTERNATIONAL TROPHY AT BROOKLANDS. 07/05/1938

PERCY MACLURE TAKES THE
CHEQUERED FLAG TO WIN THE JCC
INTERNATIONAL TROPHY AT
BROOKLANDS. 07/05/1938

JOHN COBB SITTING IN THE COCKPIT OF HIS RAILTON-MOBIL SPECIAL, WHICH WOULD BREAK THE WORLD LAND SPEED RECORD WITHIN TWO MONTHS OF THIS PICTURE BEING TAKEN. 02/07/1938

BROOKLANDS WORKERS BURN OIL OFF THE TRACK DURING A PRACTICE SESSION FOR THE JCC 200 MILE RACE. 29/08/1938

REG PARNELL, DRIVING A MASERATI
4CL, RAISES HIS HAND IN
CELEBRATION AS HE TAKES THE
CHEQUERED FLAG IN THE JCC
INTERNATIONAL TROPHY. 08/05/1947

**OPPOSITE**

PRINCE BIRABONGSE BHANUTEJ BHANUBANDH IN HIS MASERATI IN THE PITS
DURING THE JCC INTERNATIONAL TROPHY. 08/05/1947

BOB GERARD RECEIVES A HELPING HAND TO GET HIS ERA STARTED.  13/09/1948

**OPPOSITE**

ERIC OLIVER ON HIS WAY TO VICTORY
IN THE SIDECAR EVENT IN
BARCELONA. 08/04/1951

**OPPOSITE**

REG PARNELL SHOWS OFF THE
FESTIVAL OF BRITAIN TROPHY AFTER
HIS WIN IN THE FINAL. 14/05/1951

JOHN COOPER AT THE WHEEL OF
THEIR RACING CAR WITH ITS
BODYWORK STRIPPED IN SURBITON,
SURREY WITH HIS CO-DRIVER BILL
ASTON. THE FORMER MOTOR RACING
DRIVER DEVISED THE SOUPED-UP
MINI COOPER IN 1961 AND IT BECAME
THE ULTIMATE IN FOUR-WHEELED
CHIC. 15/11/1952

STIRLING MOSS SITTING IN HIS
MASERATI AFTER WINNING THE
AINTREE 200 MOTOR RACE, AT THE
DAILY TELEGRAPH INTERNATIONAL
MEETING, THE FIRST TO BE HELD AT
THE NEW TRACK BUILT BESIDE THE
FAMOUS GRAND NATIONAL COURSE.
30/05/1954

JOSE FROILAN GONZALES RECEIVES A CONGRATULATORY KISS FROM HIS WIFE AFTER WINNING THE BRITISH GRAND PRIX.

17/07/1954

STIRLING MOSS AFTER WINNING A
RACE. 04/05/1955

**OPPOSITE**

THE DRIVERS SPRINT TO THEIR CARS
AT THE START OF THE 1955 LE MANS
24 HOUR RACE. 11/06/1955

STIRLING MOSS (BEHIND CAR, R) AND PETER COLLINS (BEHIND CAR, L) ARE TOASTED DURING A PARTY AT MERCEDES BENZ
AFTER THEIR VICTORY IN THE TARGA FLORIO.    18/10/1955

MOTORCYCLE GRAND PRIX
CHAMPION MIKE 'THE BIKE'
HAILWOOD MBE, LADEN WITH HIS
COLLECTION OF TROPHIES.
12/04/1958

STIRLING MOSS IN ACTION AT THE
SILVER CITY INTERNATIONAL TROPHY
RACE AT BRANDS HATCH. 03/06/1961

**OPPOSITE**

RACE WINNER STIRLING MOSS IS THE
CENTRE OF ATTENTION AS HE HOLDS
THE TROPHY AFTER HIS VICTORY IN
THE 200-MILE RACE, DURING WHICH
HE LAPPED ALL BUT THE NEXT TWO
FINISHERS. BRANDS HATCH.
03/06/1961

RACE WINNER JIM CLARK TURNS TO
SHOW THE TROPHY TO THE CROWD
AFTER WINNING THE BRITISH GRAND
PRIX. 21/07/1962

**OPPOSITE**

ENGINEERS WORK ON THE BLUEBIRD,
WHICH HELD THE WORLD LAND
SPEED RECORD. 01/08/1962

CONSTRUCTED BY
MOTOR PANELS
COVENTRY        ENGLAND

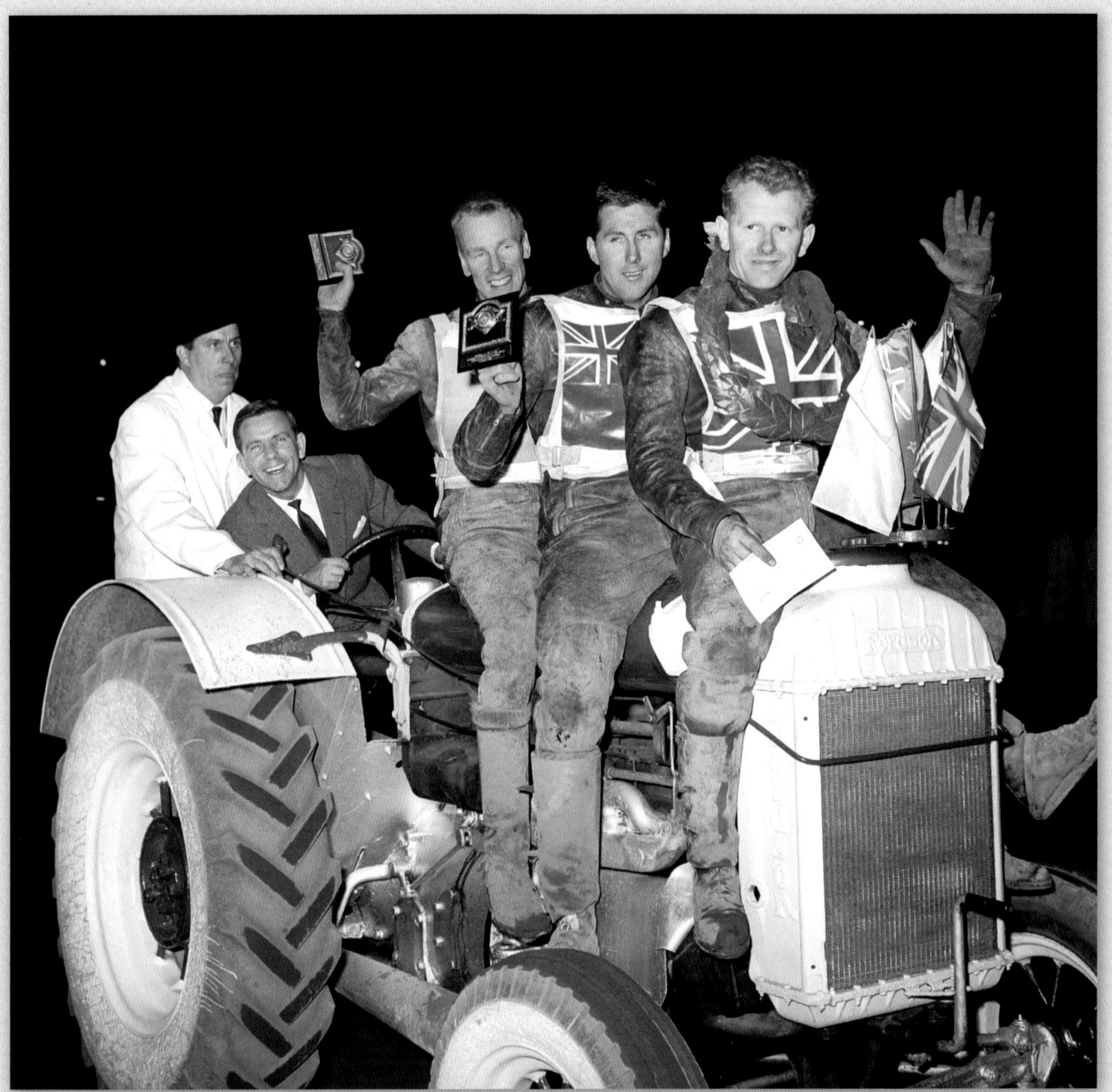

GRAHAM HILL (1) LEADS FROM
TREVOR TAYLOR (4) DURING THE
DAILY EXPRESS TROPHY AT
SILVERSTONE. 11/05/1963

**OPPOSITE**

HOLDING HIS WINNER'S CHEQUE IS PETER CRAVEN (FAR RIGHT). DRIVING THE
TRACTOR IS COMEDIAN NORMAN WISDOM WHO PRESENTED THE PRIZE AT THE
WORLD SPEEDWAY CHAMPS AT WEMBLEY STADIUM. 08/09/1962

**OPPOSITE**

MIKE HAILWOOD RETRIEVES HIS GOGGLES AFTER DROPPING THEM WHILE
CROSSING THE TRACK, FOLLOWING HIS RETIREMENT FROM THE RACE OF
CHAMPIONS AT BRANDS HATCH. 13/03/1965

JIM CLARK IS DRIVEN ON A LAP OF
HONOUR OF THE CIRCUIT TO
COMMEMORATE HIS VICTORY IN THE
INDIANAPOLIS 500. 08/06/1965

GEOFF DUKE (L) AND MIKE
HAILWOOD (R) SHOW OFF THE
TOURIST TROPHY. 16/02/1967

**OPPOSITE**

START OF THE W.D. & H.O. WILLS
TROPHY AT SILVERSTONE. 27/03/1967

JOCHEN RINDT, WINING THE WILLS TROPHY AT SILVERSTONE. 27/03/1967

MIKE HAILWOOD LEADS GIACOMO AGOSTINI, ON HIS WAY TO VICTORY IN THE 500CC RACE. CZECHOSLOVAKIAN GRAND PRIX. 28/07/1967

**OPPOSITE**

A BUGATTI ENTERED AND DRIVEN BY
E.N. FERRIS IN A CAVALCADE OF
RACING CARS OF ALL AGES ON THE
CRYSTAL PALACE CIRCUIT. 09/09/1967

HANNU MIKKOLA AND GUNNAR
PALM DRIVING THEIR FORD ESCORT
THROUGH THE DESERT OF
SOUTHERN MEXICO DURING THE
LONDON-MEXICO WORLD CUP RALLY.
14/06/1970

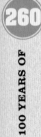

JACKIE STEWART PRESENTS THE FORMULA ONE WORLD DRIVERS'
CHAMPIONSHIP TROPHY TO JOCHEN RINDT'S WIDOW, NINA, AFTER RINDT WAS
KILLED DURING PRACTICE FOR THE ITALIAN GRAND PRIX ON 5 SEPTEMBER 1970.
17/11/1970

MIKE HAILWOOD DRIVING A SURTEES FORD TS9B DURING THE DAILY MAIL RACE OF CHAMPIONS AT BRANDS HATCH.
22/03/1972

JACKIE STEWART ON HIS WAY TO
SECOND PLACE IN THE BRITISH
GRAND PRIX. 15/07/1972

**OPPOSITE**

THE BRITISH GRAND PRIX GETS
UNDERWAY. 15/07/1972

NIKI LAUDA DRIVES AROUND BRANDS
HATCH IN HIS FERRARI DURING THE
QUALIFYING STAGES OF THE BRITISH
GRAND PRIX. 19/07/1974

**OPPOSITE**

AMERICAN STUNT MAN EVEL KNIEVEL DURING A DISPLAY AT WEMBLEY
STADIUM. HE CRASHED AFTER ATTEMPTING A MOTORCYCLE LEAP OVER 13
BUSES. HE WAS BADLY INJURED AND TAKEN TO HOSPITAL. 26/05/1975

JAMES HUNT DRIVING A FORK LIFT
TRUCK. 01/07/1975

**OPPOSITE**

BARRY SHEENE CELEBRATES VICTORY
IN THE 500CC GRAND PRIX WITH A
BOTTLE OF CHAMPAGNE. 10/08/1975

FORMER WORLD CHAMPION MIKE HAILWOOD WAVES TO THE CROWD AS HE IS DRIVEN ON A LAP OF HONOUR. 10/08/1975

FORMULA ONE WORLD CHAMPION JAMES HUNT IS SURROUNDED BY HORDES
OF AUTOGRAPH HUNTERS. 08/11/1976

FORMULA ONE WORLD CHAMPION JAMES HUNT IS SURROUNDED BY HORDES
OF AUTOGRAPH HUNTERS. 08/11/1976

**FOLLOWING PAGE**

CARLOS REUTEMANN TAKES THE
CHEQUERED FLAG AS HE WINS THE
BRITISH GRAND PRIX. 16/07/1978

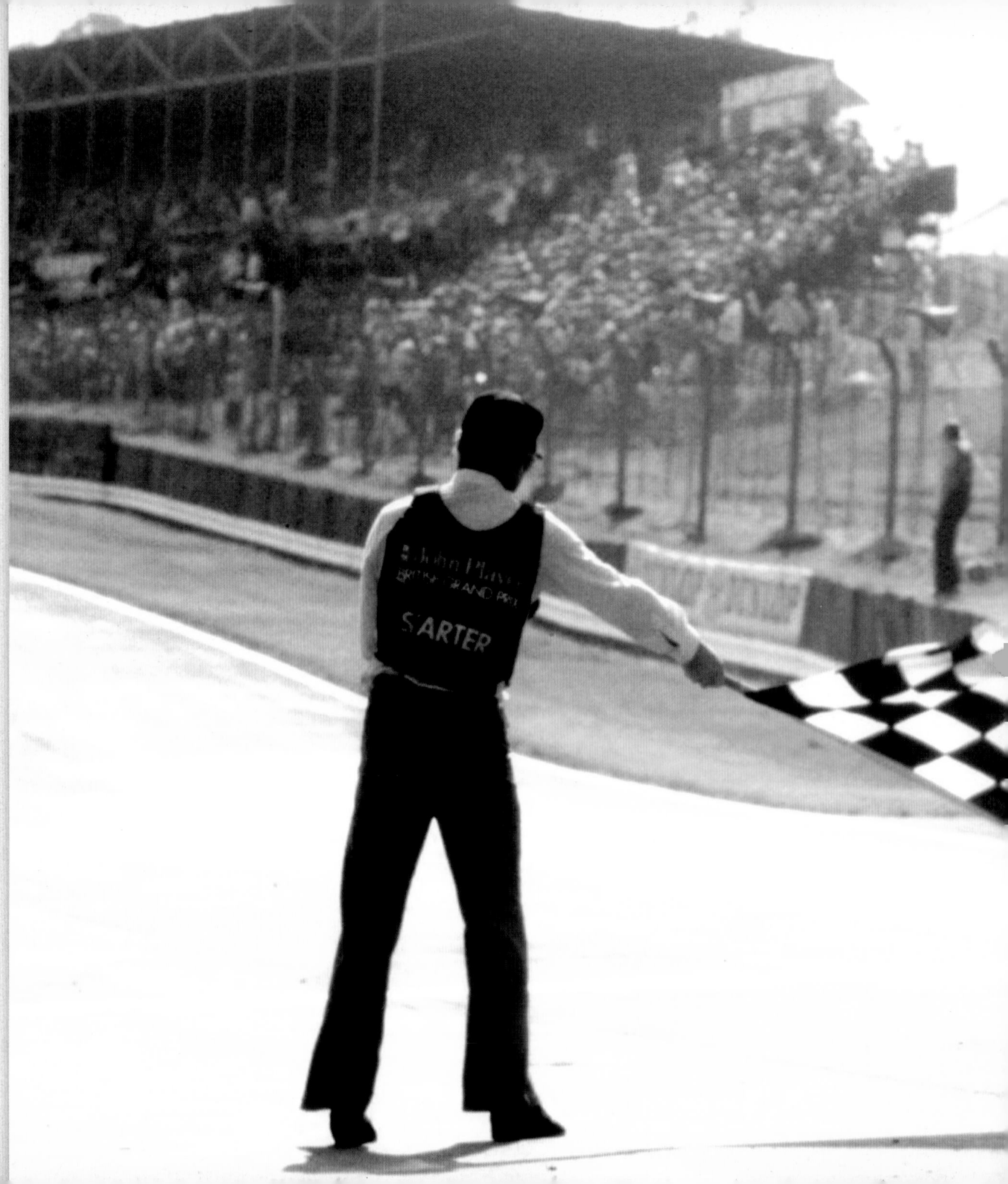
STARTER

AT THE PRACTICE FOR THE BRITISH GRAND PRIX AT SILVERSTONE, AUSTRALIA'S ALAN JONES REMOVES HIS PROTECTIVE
BALACLAVA AFTER GOING ROUND THE 2.93 MILE CIRCUIT AT AN AVERAGE SPEED OF 146MPH, TAKING ONE MINUTE, 11.88
SECONDS, 7 SECONDS FASTER THAN JAMES HUNT'S OFFICIAL RECORD. 12/07/1979

CLAY REGAZZONI HOLDS THE TROPHY AFTER DRIVING A SAUDIA-WILLIAMS TO VICTORY AT THE BRITISH GRAND PRIX AT SILVERSTONE. ON THE RIGHT IS JEAN-PIERRE JARIER, WHO TOOK THIRD PLACE IN A CANDY TYRRELL. 15/07/1979

BARRY SHEENE IN ACTION IN THE
500CC GRAND PRIX RACE AT
SILVERSTONE. 12/08/1979

EDDIE KIDD PERFORMS A JUMP OVER
FIVE SPECTATORS' CARS. 19/05/1981

**OPPOSITE**

BRIAN HENTON GETS OUT OF HIS
TOLEMAN CANDY AS IT BURSTS INTO
FLAMES IN PRACTICE AT THE BRITISH
GRAND PRIX. 17/07/1981

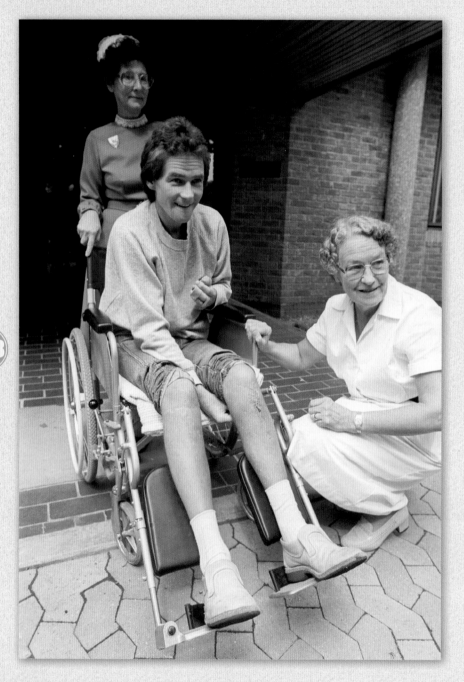

PHYSIOTHERAPIST BETSY NEWTON (R) CHECKS ON THE CONDITION OF BARRY SHEENE AS HE LEAVES HOSPITAL TO CONTINUE HIS REHABILITATION AT HOME, HAVING SUFFERED TWO BROKEN LEGS AND A BROKEN ARM IN A CRASH AT SILVERSTONE IN JULY. 20/08/1982

NIGEL MANSELL THROWS HIS CAP INTO A THRONG OF FANS AFTER FINISHING SECOND IN THE BRITISH GRAND PRIX.

10/07/1988

AYRTON SENNA, MCLAREN HONDA,

AT THE BRITISH GRAND PRIX.

16/07/1989

**OPPOSITE**

MCLAREN DRIVER ALAIN PROST
CELEBRATES WINNING THE BRITISH
GRAND PRIX. 16/07/1989

GERHARD BERGER, NIGEL MANSELL
AND AYRTON SENNA SHOW SIGNS
OF EXHAUSTION ON THE WINNERS'
PODIUM AT THE PORTUGUESE
GRAND PRIX. 01/10/1992

DAMON HILL'S WILLIAMS RENAULT
DRIVES OVER A GRAFFITI TRIBUTE TO
THE LATE AYRTON SENNA AT SPA
DURING THE BELGIAN GRAND PRIX.
29/08/1994

GWYNDAF EVANS LAUNCHES INTO
THE AIR AFTER COLLIDING WITH A
TREE STUMP AT THE CHATSWORTH
HOUSE STAGE OF THE BRITISH RALLY.
24/11/1996

**OPPOSITE**

THE NEW WORLD CHAMPION DAMON
HILL (R) CELEBRATES WITH THE OLD
WORLD CHAMPION MICHAEL
SCHUMACHER. 13/10/1996

DAVID COULTHARD CELEBRATES
WINNING THE ITALIAN GRAND PRIX.
07/09/1997

**OPPOSITE**

NICKY GRIST (L) AND COLIN MCRAE
(R) CELEBRATE WINNING THE RAC
RALLY. 25/11/1997

FERRARI BOSS JEAN TODT (C) WITH EDDIE IRVINE (L) AND MICHAEL SCHUMACHER (R) AT THE ARGENTINIAN GRAND PRIX.
12/04/1998

DAMON HILL CELEBRATES HIS
VICTORY IN THE BELGIAN GRAND
PRIX. 30/08/1998

**FOLLOWING PAGE**

THE FERRARI TEAM CELEBRATE
MICHAEL SCHUMACHER'S WIN AS HE
TAKES THE CHEQUERED FLAG IN THE
ITALIAN GRAND PRIX. TEAMMATE
EDDIE IRVINE FINISHED SECOND.
13/09/1998